I SPY
DINOSAUR
WITH MY LITTLE EYE

For Further Communication:
Email: azulancreatives@gmail.com
Facebook: fb.com/azulancreatives
Website: www.azulancreatives.com

This Book Belongs To

This book is especially designed for the Dinosaur lover toddlers and preschoolers.
It will increase their visual ability, problem solving skills and concentration.

Best Wishes!

- Azulan Publication

I Spy with my little eye something beginning with.....

A is for

ALLOSAURUS

I Spy with my little eye something beginning with.....

B is for

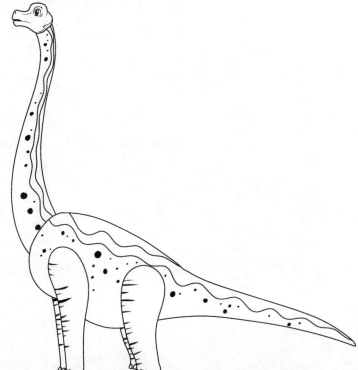

BACTROSAURUS

I Spy with my little eye something beginning with.....

C
is for

CEDARPELTA

I Spy with my little eye something beginning with.....

D is for

DACENTRURUS

I Spy with my little eye something beginning with......

E is for

EOLAMBIA

I Spy with my little eye something beginning with......

F is for

FUKUIRAPTOR

I Spy with my little eye something beginning with......

G is for

GASOSAURUS

I Spy with my little eye something beginning with......

H is for

HESPEROSAURUS

I Spy with my little eye something beginning with.....

I is for

IGUANODON

I Spy with my little eye something beginning with......

J is for

JOBARIA

I Spy with my little eye something beginning with.....

K is for

KENTROSAURUS

I Spy with my little eye something beginning with.....

L is for

LURDUSAURUS

I Spy with my little eye something beginning with......

M is for

MUSSAURUS

I Spy with my little eye something beginning with.....

N is for

NOMINGIA

I Spy with my little eye something beginning with.....

O is for

OURANOSAURUS

I Spy with my little eye something beginning with.....

P is for

PARASAUROLOPHUS

I Spy with my little eye something beginning with.....

Q is for

QUAESITOSAURUS

I Spy with my little eye something beginning with.....

R is for

REBBACHISAURUS

I Spy with my little eye something beginning with.....

S is for

SPINOSAURUS

I Spy with my little eye something beginning with.....

T

T is for

TTYRANNOSAURUS

I Spy with my little eye something beginning with.....

U is for

UTAHRAPTOR

I Spy with my little eye something beginning with.....

V  is for

VELOCIRAPTOR

I Spy with my little eye something beginning with.....

W is for

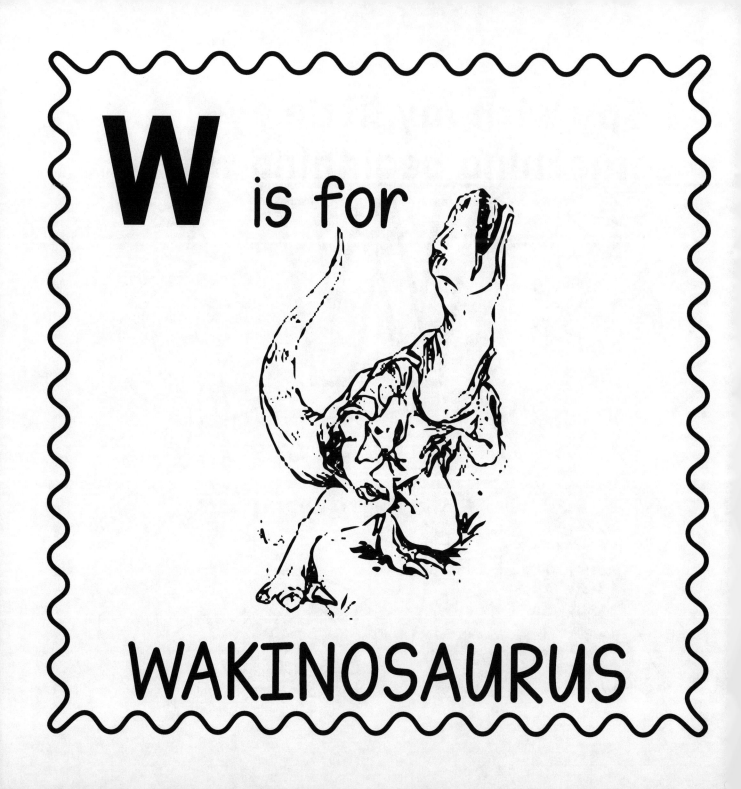

WAKINOSAURUS

I Spy with my little eye something beginning with.....

X  is for

XIAOTINGIA

I Spy with my little eye something beginning with......

Y is for

YINLONG

I Spy with my little eye something beginning with......

Made in the USA
Middletown, DE
03 October 2023

40117474R00033